Outcome Thinking

Framework-Tools and Tips

K V Vishwanathan

Copyright © 2024 by K V Vishwanathan

All rights reserved.

This book or any portion thereof may not be reproduced or used in any manner whatsoever without the express written permission of the respective writer of the respective content except for the use of brief quotations in a book review.

The writer of the respective work holds sole responsibility for the originality of the content and The Write Order is not responsible in any way whatsoever.

Printed in India

ISBN: 978-93-5776-810-8

First Printing, 2024

The Write Order
A division of Nasadiya Technologies Private Ltd.
Koramangala, Bengaluru
Karnataka-560029

THE WRITE ORDER PUBLICATIONS.

www.thewriteorder.com

Edited by Anagha Somanakoppa

Typeset by MAP Systems, Bengaluru

Book Cover designed by Nikhil Kamath

Publishing Consultant - Aishwarya Wanjari

Dedication

This initiative is dedicated to:

My late parents and guardians who were the essence of kindness and courage; who gave me the freedom of choice to decide what I wanted to do in life.

This book is dedicated to all the mentors, guides, teachers, managers of different organisations
I have worked with who helped shape the thought on what is possible and what can be made possible.

Contents

Acknowledgements ix

Foreword xi

Chapter 1
Outcome Thinking - an introduction 1

Chapter 2
Problems 5

Chapter 3
The Drive Framework - an overview 11

Chapter 4
Defining 13

Chapter 5
Neurological Levels 15

Chapter 6
Reframing 31

Chapter 7
Six steps in Reframing 35

Chapter 8
A Study on Reframing 43

Chapter 9
Contaminated Vocabulary 47

Chapter 10
The Six Ps of Reframing 53

Chapter 11
The Perception of Reality Map 59

Chapter 12
Metaphor..67

Chapter 13
Problem-Solving through metaphors 73

Chapter 14
Ideation 75

Chapter 15
Validation 79

Chapter 16
The Six Steps of Validation 81

Chapter 17
Experimenting...85

Chapter 18
Powerful Questions Framework 89

Acknowledgements

I thank the developers of Neurolinguistic Programming Dr Richard Bandler and John Grinder; all the tutors, trainers, authors, writers and Practitioners of Neurolinguistic Programming, my friends and different clients with whom I had interacted over the past 30 years who helped directly and indirectly in the writing of this book.

I thank Subha Tharuvai Nilakantan my former school mate, a good friend and herself an author of two books for the apt illustrations, Mitul bose for helping me in editing and above all my colleagues at Nivritti Associates and my family for the support and accommodating my time in coming out with this book.

Foreword

"Outcome Thinking: Framework, Tools, and Tips" is an important new book by K.V. Vishwanathan.

This book is a welcomed addition to the growing body of work on Outcome Thinking, which offers an alternative approach to achieving tangible results by focusing on outcomes rather than output or process.

We often expend excessive energy on operations and outputs while neglecting outcomes—the goals, activities, and deliverables that best serve a need. What greater purpose or mission could there be for a business and its team than to understand and cater to customer needs, emphasizing outcomes over outputs?

In this book, Vishwanathan elegantly explores this concept, utilizing various frameworks such as DRIVE (Chapter 3) and Reframing (Chapter 6) to help readers implement the concept effectively.

"Outcome Thinking: Framework, Tools, and Tips" is interspersed with small exercises and illustrations, making it easier for readers to grasp the concepts presented in the book.

Chapters like "Problem Solving Through Metaphors" (Chapter 13) and "Ideation" (Chapter 14) serve as examples of conveying messages through simple exercises.

Vishwanathan guides readers through logically organized ideas, with sections on Validation (Chapters 15 and 16), culminating in the concluding sections on Experiments and Questions (Chapters 17 and 18), bringing us to a logical conclusion.

This book serves as a practical demonstration of Outcome Thinking, as Vishwanathan illustrates how to start with ideas, refine and validate them, and ultimately achieve clear, targeted learning outcomes.

"Outcome Thinking: Framework, Tools, and Tips" is likely to appeal to both newcomers seeking an introductory treatise on Outcome Thinking and professional practitioners and trainers interested in the subject.

Ananth Ramachandran
Senior Banker
Singapore

I am very pleased and honored to write the Foreword for this book. First and foremost, I would like to warmly congratulate K.V. Viswanathan on this publication, which is a wealth of information and expertise.

During a recent Future of Work event, attended by over 1,000 professionals from around the globe, I made a statement in my keynote address: outcome-thinking can be invoked when contemplating the future of all professions. Our stakeholders value us for the outcomes we deliver. When these outcomes can be reliably achieved in new, demonstrably more cost-effective, efficient, or convenient ways, especially in today's age of AI, we should anticipate disruption in our lives and work. Therefore, outcome thinking is crucial for constant reinvention.

We all labor under a tyranny of tasks, which are the building blocks of work and productivity. However, an outcome is more than a blueprint; it represents the most enriched version of a goal. An outcome is a goal that tells a story—to ourselves and to others—about where we want to arrive.

I am confident that this book will be of great interest to many, aiding them in planning and executing their organizational strategies and maximizing their commercial value.

As K.V. Viswanathan aptly states, in an imperfect world, challenges are ever-present. You do not have to seek them out; they will find you. Many leaders get lost in the labyrinth of problem analysis—investigating the reasons, costs, consequences, and assigning blame. Outcome thinking represents a change in mindset. Thinking in outcomes can help an organization focus and clarify its mission by compelling it to explicitly state and communicate its goals, particularly to its stakeholders.

The challenges in today's workplace are both daunting and intriguing. People are diligently working on them, dedicated to developing new delivery methods and offering fresh solutions to keep pace with our ever-changing world. In this new era of global interconnectivity, interdependence, and Generative AI, outcome thinking will help companies discover hidden opportunities in core, adjacent, and emerging markets. It will enable the capture of larger market shares by positioning current offerings alongside the opportunities that exist in a market.

Outcome thinkers create products that transform businesses, innovate, and connect people. They deliver because they make outcomes the cornerstone of their thinking and decision-making.

This book will be an invaluable resource for many and is highly recommended for all those involved in designing and delivering organizational results in an increasingly competitive and complex business world.

Girish Ganesan
Senior HR Executive
CIO Views Top 10 HR Leaders to Follow, and 2019 Canada's Top 40 under 40

Over the last fifteen years, I have witnessed Vish sharing his wisdom with numerous individuals through various workshops. Vish is an expert in NLP, and his frameworks have significantly enhanced the effectiveness of countless people. It is a pleasure to see that he has distilled all his vast experience into a book, which will help spread the message far and wide.

I particularly appreciate many aspects of the book, one example being the chapter on 'reframing.' I have personally and professionally benefited greatly from reframing, and I am confident that readers will also find this framework, among many others, highly valuable.

Utilizing these templates and frameworks can empower individuals to realize their full potential. The book holds many other valuable insights waiting to be discovered by its readers.

Vikram Bector,
Director and Group CHRO
Welspun World.

Chapter 1

Outcome Thinking
an introduction

Outcome Thinking is a shift in mindset. It is a way of thinking that can transform your business by focusing on the impact your products/services have on your clients, rather than solely on the products/services themselves. In other words, it involves envisioning a describable future result that stimulates action by engaging our senses, emotions, and logical mind. Outcome-oriented thinking directs attention to questions like: What results can we achieve with our products and services?

The primary objective of the result-led approach in an organizational context is to reduce time-to-market. Often, many organizations lack a clear vision of their desired achievements and instead concentrate on product improvement. The more specific you can be about your desired outcomes, the greater your chances of reaching them.

Outcome thinking helps you sharpen your focus, eliminate tasks that do not add value, provide opportunities for course correction, and increase overall effectiveness. It also enables better communication with your team and empowers them by allowing them to determine the best way forward. When you have a clear destination in mind, it becomes much easier to develop the right plan to reach it, don't you think?

To begin, let's use the term "outcome" instead of "goal" or "objective" to describe the desired solutions/results. An outcome is also more specific and measurable than a goal, objective, or solution. Thinking about outcomes is essential in management, as it provides direction and purpose for your actions and gives you control over the path you wish to pursue.

There are two important points to consider regarding this novel way of thinking

Whether you set outcomes or not, you are always obtaining results; however, they may not align with what you have in mind. The way you establish outcomes is crucial—they should be realistic, motivating, and achievable.

Outcomes have become widely recognized in management, largely due to the writings of Peter Drucker. Drucker believed that business leaders should embrace a performance-driven mindset, displaying high levels of moral and ethical integrity in their actions while focusing on "results," or outcomes. Setting outcomes is not just a task to be done at specific times; it represents an entire way of thinking. Outcome thinking entails being focused on what you want to achieve.

The opposite of outcome thinking is problem thinking, which fixates on identifying what is wrong in a particular situation and seeking solutions. In an imperfect world, challenges are always present, and there is no need to seek them out actively—they will naturally arise. Many leaders get lost in the maze of problem analysis, trying to determine the reasons, costs, consequences, and who to blame.

On the other hand, outcome thinking embraces three elements

- Your present situation—where you currently are, stuck in your problem state.

- Your desired situation—where you want to be, where you want to go. Asking this question provides direction and guidance.

- Your resources—how you will move from one situation to another This helps you assess the resources you already have and what additional resources you may need to transition from the current state to the desired state.

Outcomes are expressed in a positive manner since they direct you towards something you want to achieve rather than moving away from something you want to avoid.

Instead of asking, "What do I not want?" ask, "What do I want?"

Adopting an approach of outcome thinking helps orient your organization/department towards achieving desired outcomes and convinces internal and external stakeholders that what you/they are doing is effective.

To understand how it works, we need to delve into the process of thinking about outcomes, exploring the finer nuances and challenges. The following chapters will assist you in enabling, defining, aligning, and measuring your best possible outcomes.

Chapter 2

Problems

A problem or challenge can be seen as an opportunity or a doorway to breakthrough innovation. Most problems are connected to attitudes, which are a reflection of your personality and can be shaped by your upbringing and environment. Attitudes are born out of an understanding of a given situation, and when the knowledge of a situation changes, our attitude also changes.

For example, let's say one of your colleagues opens a packet of sweets during a lunch break and offers you one. You refuse to have the sweet and say no due to your attitude towards it. Your attitude is based on the knowledge that the sweet contains sugar, which you avoid because of your dietary restrictions. Your colleague, unaware of this, tries to persuade you to have it, but you once again decline. At this point, you may hear comments like, 'What an attitude he has!'

However, when your colleague tells you that this sweet was made at home by his Mother and was offered to the deity, you accept it. What changed your mind? You accepted the sweet based on the *veracity* of the statement that it was made at home, prepared by his mother, and offered to the deity. The situation suddenly changed, and what had been unacceptable so far became acceptable. However, the knowledge that the sweet contains sugar and might harm you remains the same. In this case, the attitude changes from unknown to known.

Another example is seen in the ritual of reverential salutation performed by Indian classical dancers on the stage where they perform. Saluting the stage displays an attitude that is linked to one's culture. When performing on stage, it is an act of reverence for Nature and Mother Earth.

It is clear that a synergistic attitude and problem-solving skills could solve 90% of all our problems. Therefore, it is important to understand problem-solving better.

Application of creativity in problem solving

Educational research reveals that many people display a great deal of creativity until the age of 5. Unfortunately, their creative output diminishes as they mature. This can be due to many factors that inhibit creativity, particularly in the process of formal education. Therefore, all of us need assistance in helping our innate creativity resurface.

Secondly, let us understand how creativity helps in problem-solving

To begin with, some myths about creativity need to be debunked.

Myth no. 1: Creativity cannot be studied.

Reality: Research on creativity began in the 1950s, and laboratory studies started in the 1970s. Research on creativity continues.

Myth no. 2: Creativity is rare.

Reality: The neural processes that underlie creativity are universal.

Myth no. 3: Creativity cannot be learned.

Reality: Everyone can learn to express greater creativity.

Myth no. 4: Creativity is mysterious.

Reality: The process of creativity can seem mysterious because feelings of frustration and confusion accompany it.

Myth no. 5: Creativity is in your right brain.

Reality: No specific neural location for creativity has been found so far.

Myth no. 6: Only people with high IQs are creative.

Reality: No study shows that a particular degree of intelligence is necessary for creativity.

To apply creativity to problem-solving, you need to know your creative potential. There are many online tests available to assess creative ability. Find out where your strengths lie and which areas you need to work on.

Most of us get brilliant ideas every day, whether while traveling, waiting for someone, or engaging in activities. However, we often fail to note down or record these ideas, and over time, they fade from memory.

How do we improve creativity?

1. One method to improve creativity is to capture these ideas on paper or by recording voice notes on your phone. Leverage technology to capture new ideas, which can help address challenges and problems in business and life.

2. The second tip for improving creativity is to expand your skills and knowledge base. Many of us stop reading after school or university. However, learning should be a continuous process. Stop limiting yourself to reading only material directly related to your field. There is always a possibility of getting ideas or learning a new approach from sources unrelated to your field. For example, you can learn mentoring tips from a gardening book, similar to how a gardener helps a flower blossom by watering or removing weeds.

3. The third tip for improving creativity is to seek challenges in life rather than fall into a monotonous routine. If

you work in an organization, seek challenging tasks within your role or consider transitioning to a different department or function. Working with different types of people and cultures within the same organization enhances creativity. From an organizational perspective, consider diversifying into a different domain, expertise, product, or service.

4. The fourth tip is to change your physical and social environment regularly. Looking at situations from different perspectives helps develop flexibility. For example, rearranging your furniture at home every six months can stimulate a change in your thought process. When facing a challenging situation, change your perspective and try to look at it from a different point of view. For example, when you have a conflict with your partner, client, or friend, pivot and consider an arbitrary view, a third perspective. This may provide completely new insight.

5. The fifth tip is to face and manage failures. Many experts have stated that failure is a stepping stone to success. In outcome thinking, consider failure as feedback rather than a negative situation. Approach the situation or problem differently based on the feedback received. Remember that there are no failures, only results. Treat it as feedback that "approach A" has resulted in an undesired outcome, and to achieve the desired result, you need to adopt approaches B, C, D, or E.

Chapter 3

The Drive Framework
an overview

"If I had an hour to solve a problem, I would spend 55 minutes thinking about the problem and 5 minutes thinking about solutions."

- Albert Einstein

What is the DRIVE framework, and how does it help address business challenges and problems?

The DRIVE Framework is designed to assist organizations in navigating uncertainty and challenges by examining socio-economic events and their potential future impact.

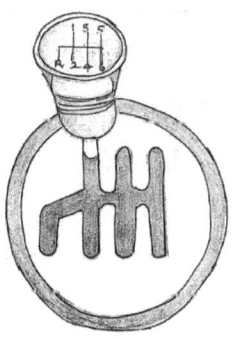

above figure: an example of a gear box

In my thirty-plus years of experience in the corporate world, working, teaching, and facilitating, I have realized that when most organizations face a challenge, they immediately dive into solution mode. This rush could be due to time constraints, work pressure, or other external pressures, often without devoting time to understanding why the problem occurred and who it is affecting. Without comprehending the root cause, finding a solution becomes difficult, and even if one is found, it may turn out to be suboptimal.

The following framework aims to help discover the origins of a problem or challenge and chart a path towards a solution. This framework is known as DRIVE, an acronym representing:

- Defining
- Reframing
- Ideating
- Validating
- Experimenting

It also signifies the drive for solutions. Subsequent chapters delve into each letter of the acronym in detail, providing a deeper understanding of the concept.

Chapter 4

Defining
R
I
V
E

When you are faced with a challenge, you need to go deeper into the issue and discover more about it. Ask the following questions to get the full picture:

→ Who does the problem affect?

→ What impact does it have on people?

→ When does the problem occur?

→ Where does it occur?

→ Why does it occur?

→ How does it affect you?

When you have answers to these Five Ws and H questions, you will start finding the path to the solution, even before venturing into ideation. For deeper clarity, let us understand the framework of the Neurological Levels, which help with each of the five Ws and the H.

Chapter 5

Neurological Levels

The neurological level is a very valuable tool that assists in organizing thinking, information gathering, and communication. This model allows us to understand in a clear, structured manner what, where, how, when, and why a situation/problem/challenge arose.

We build relationships with ourselves and others on different levels. This may have a subtle effect on how we diagnose, think, feel, and view our problems or organizational challenges.

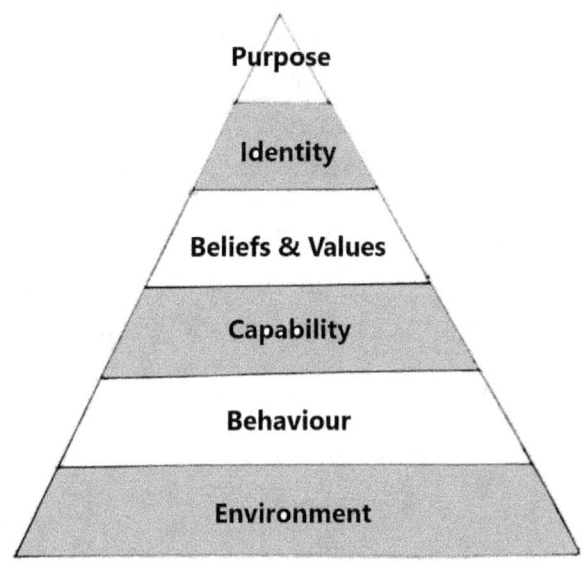

1. The first level is the environment (the 'where' and 'when'):

The environment encompasses the physical place we find ourselves in and the people we are associated with. You have probably heard people attribute their success to being in the right place at the right time, indicating the significance of the environment. At this level, shared circumstances play a crucial role in building rapport.

For example, when facing a particular challenge, it is essential to pinpoint precisely where and when you encounter it.

2. The second level is behavior (the 'what'):

This level involves our specific, conscious actions—what we do. Behavior encompasses both thoughts and actions. Our actions are not random; they are purposeful and aimed at achieving specific outcomes, although these purposes may not always be clear, even to us.

You may desire to change your behavior and reactions to various situations. However, changing behavior can be challenging because it is closely intertwined with other neurological levels. Therefore, it is important to analyze your actions when confronted with a situation or problem.

When reflecting on how you respond to similar situations or problems, closely observe your actions. This self-awareness can help you identify elements to avoid, paving the way for a solution.

3. The third level is capability (the 'how'):

At this level, we focus on skills. We possess both innate skills like walking and talking and consciously learned skills such as mathematics, sports, or music. Behaviour that we frequently practice becomes consistent, automatic, and habitual. This includes both thinking strategies and physical skills. When someone describes their success as a fluke, they attribute it to the behavioural level, suggesting that they don't view it as consistently repeatable—it has not yet become a capability.

This level enables you to determine whether the current situation or problem is due to a skills gap among team members or whether a skills gap exists on the client's end. An in-depth inquiry will reveal the true reasons, ultimately aiding you in finding a path to a solution.

4. The fourth level is beliefs and values (the 'why'):

This level delves into what is important to us. Beliefs and values significantly influence our lives, serving as both permissions and prohibitions. If you desire to develop specific skills but believe you cannot, this belief becomes a self-fulfilling prophecy. If you do not value something, you lack motivation to acquire it.

We are also capable of holding conflicting beliefs and values, leading to actions that contradict each other over time.

Ask yourself:

- Are these challenges arising because of specific or limiting beliefs you hold?

- Is there a conflict of values contributing to this specific issue?

- Do the values of your clients, team, or organization align?

- Is there a disconnect between what you believe and what your customers or team members believe?

Asking these questions can provide valuable insights and guide you toward a solution.

5. The fifth level is identity (the 'who'):

Have you ever heard someone say, 'I am just not that kind of person'? This is an identity statement. Identity encompasses your sense of self, your core beliefs, and the values that define who you are and your life's mission. Your identity is highly resilient, yet you can build, develop, and change it.

Similarly, you might hear representatives of organizations say, 'We are not that kind of organization.' This, too, is an identity statement. Identity represents the organization's core sense of who they are, their core beliefs and values, and their mission. The organization's identity is very resilient, but it can be built, developed, and changed.

Here, you may need to conduct some inquiries to determine how well the identity level is linked to your problem:

- Who in your organization faces this business challenge?

- Is it every employee or only some who are facing it?

- Is it specific to certain individuals within your department?

- If the latter, are there particular people who are encountering this challenge?

- Do 'all' your customers encounter challenges with your product, or is it only 'some of the customers'?

- Does the problem arise due to a specific person within the organization or outside it?

- Are 'you,' the one reading this, the source of the problem? Are 'you' causing the problem?

These questions will provide more clarity on who is contributing to the problem. It may not be the individual's intention to cause a problem, but it might occur due to a belief or value conflict with the team, the organization as a whole, or a customer.

6. Finally, the sixth level is purpose:

This level is about your connection with others and a purpose that extends beyond your identity.

Ask:

- Why is the situation you are facing a problem at all?

- Is the mission and vision of your organization contributing to this problem?

- Could the mission or vision itself be the problem?

- Is the organization's purpose a contributing factor to the problem?

Robert Dilts (1991), the creator of the Neurological Levels in Neurolinguistic Programming (NLP), states, "For one level to be higher than another, the higher one has to be about the lower, and the lower has to be a member of the class of the higher. When that happens, the higher level will govern, modulate, and organize the lower."

"In our brain structure, language, and perceptual systems, there are natural hierarchies or levels of experiences. The effect of each level is to organize and control the information on the level below it. Changing something on an upper level would necessarily change things on the lower levels, and changing something on a lower level could affect the upper levels."

"Logical Levels: an internal hierarchy in which each level is progressively more psychologically encompassing and impactful." (Dilts, Epstein, Dilts, 1991).

Five components that enable us to begin building an operational definition of logical levels include:

- Hierarchies of experience

- Higher levels organizing and controlling information on lower levels

- The modulation effect of the system necessarily works downward

- The modulation effect of the system does not necessarily work upward

- Higher levels are more encompassing and impactful than lower levels

Quoting Robert Dilts again: Logical typing occurs where there is a discontinuity (as opposed to continuity), as with the hierarchies between levels of classification. This kind of discontinuity is exemplified by:

a) in mathematics, by the restriction that a class cannot be a member of itself, nor can one of the members be the class.

b) in logic, by the solution to the classic logical paradox, 'This statement is false.' (If the statement is true, it is false, and if it is false, then it is true, and so on.) The actual truth value of the statement is of a different logical type than the statement itself.

c) in behaviour, by the fact that the reinforcement rules for exploration in animals are of a completely different nature than those for the process of testing that occurs in the act of exploration."

The informational effects between levels and types can be called feedback.

"Differences of the same or different logical type interacting at different levels (hierarchical or logical, respectively) will result in the modulation of the difference on the lower level."

The Language of Levels

The structure of any team emerges from these five levels:

→ Where it is situated

→ What it does

→ What it can do

→ What is important to it and its identity

Business problems can occur at any level. How do you know which level to address?

One way is to listen to the exact words people use when describing their concerns—not just the words but the emphasis they put on them.

Suppose someone says to you, "I cannot do that **here**." Clearly, what they are telling you is not that they cannot do it, but that they cannot do it <u>in this environment.</u>

On the other hand, supposing they say, "I cannot do that here." What they are telling you is not that it cannot be done here, but that "<u>they</u>" cannot do it here.

You may well have heard somebody say, "I **cannot** do that here." They are actually telling you about a belief they have. They are saying that they do not believe they can do it.

We can map out all five logical levels using these same sentences:

IDENTITY	I cannot do that here/ I cannot solve this problem This means I cannot solve this problem but SOMEBODY ELSE can
BELIEFS AND VALUES	I <u>CANNOT</u> do that here/ I CANNOT solve this problem This means something prevents me from solving this problem
CAPABILITY	I cannot <u>DO</u> that here/ I cannot <u>SOLVE</u> this problem This means I don't have the ability to solve this problem
BEHAVIOUR	I cannot do <u>THAT</u> here/ I cannot solve <u>THIS</u> problem This means I cannot solve THIS problem but can solve other problems.
ENVIRONMENT	I cannot do that <u>HERE</u>/ I cannot solve this problem <u>HERE</u>

This means I could have solved this problem if it were in a different place, but not in this environment. I could have solved this problem if it were in my previous organization, but not in this one.

Let us look at a few more examples of business challenges using these levels.

1

Identity	We are a good team.
Belief	Taking the advanced course in customer service helped the team greatly.
Capability	Our team is excellent when it comes to communication skills.
Behaviour	A couple of the team members did not perform well in this year's appraisal.

2

Environment	The team works well here.
Identity	Each team member runs his or her unit like an entrepreneur.
Belief	The team should be allowed to maximize profits without interference from the government
Capability	As a leader, I delegate effectively to achieve results.
Behaviour	I expect you to be on time for our next meeting.

3

Environment	This open-plan office has improved communication.
Identity	We are not the sort of company that would use that appraisal system.
Belief	It is not important to be able to do that.
Capability	We have not been able to implement that decision yet.
Behavior	Our team handled the customer complaint very efficiently.
Environment	The interview room was cold.

4

Identity	The client representative is very self-centered.
Belief	We cannot have what we want.
Capability	The team is very good when it comes to bonding and collaborating.
Behavior	Let us visit our clients in person and find out what their requirements are.
Environment	Why don't you keep your workstation tidy?

Logical levels hold a pivotal position in strategic planning. When you are devising a change strategy, it is crucial to consider all five levels and understand the potential impact of any proposed changes. Unfortunately, a comprehensive 360-degree approach to problem-solving is often rare.

Ensuring clarity across all levels when planning a change entails understanding the consequences of your actions. Far too often, individuals focus solely on one or two levels, and as a result, they are caught off guard when implementing a plan that appears flawless on paper. Therefore, it is essential that whenever you set goals, objectives, or seek to address business challenges, you thoroughly examine all the neurological levels.

Application of the logical levels framework in outcome thinking

Now that we have a clear idea about the neurological levels, the next step is to utilize their structured framework in outcome thinking. To understand the what, where, how, when, and why of the problem/challenge.

Vision and Mission

Why	What and why we think is important,	Purpose
Who	Who we are (Role)	Identity
What	What we believe	Values/ Beliefs
How	What we can do	Capabilities
What	Actions/ Reactions	Behaviour
WhereWhen and with Whom	External Context	Environment

An activity on problems using neurological levels

1. Consider a current problem/issue that you are facing.

2. What level does it seem to stem from?

3. Where will you intervene?

4. Would it be preferable to stay on the same level as the problem, or do you need to address a different level?

5. Test your solution for possible consequences at all five levels.

Further Practice

1. Choose a client meeting and identify the logical level your client is talking from.

2. Watch a news channel, a drama, or a play on TV with the sound down and guess at which level the speaker is talking. This way, you will get used to picking up visual clues as well. Notice particular hand gestures. When you see a hand go to the person's upper chest region, you are almost certainly seeing an identity-level statement.

3. Take one logical level every day and watch and listen to how many examples you come across.

An activity on neurological levels to complete after reading this book

There will have been times in your life when you were a leader/problem solver, maybe in school/college/home/function/workplace/projects where you would have solved some problem.

1. Think about your ENVIRONMENT when you acted as a leader/problem solver.

2. What situation were you in?

3. Who was there?

4. What made it easy for you to lead those people and solve the problem?

5. What did you do? Think of the actual BEHAVIOR.

6. What did you think?

7. What actions did you take?

8. What SKILLS did you use?

9. Were there particular ways of thinking that you employed?

10. Did you use any physical skills?

11. How were you CAPABLE of being a leader or a problem solver?

12. What did you BELIEVE when you were a leader in that situation?

13. What was true for you at that moment?

14. What did you VALUE?

15. What was important to you then?

16. WHO were you then?

17. Who are you now?

18. Are you different? If so, how?

19. How do all the things you have discovered about being a leader fit in with who you are?

20. What has changed?

21. What has not changed?

Chapter 6

D
Reframing
I
V
E

The next acronym of the DRIVE framework refers to Reframing. Life has many ups and downs. We do not always get what we desire; on the other hand, we end up getting many things we did not actually want. Many a time, when we go through a difficult time, we ask, 'Why me?'

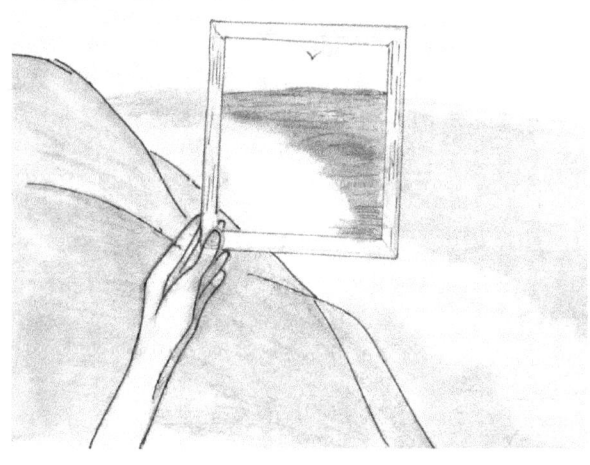

This is where the mind plays a critical role. If we keep replaying these thoughts repeatedly in our minds, they can become our reality because we start believing in them. One technique that can help in such situations is changing our frame of mind. This is akin to swapping the frame of a family photo from a wooden one to a golden one. The photo itself remains the same, but the emotions associated with it can change. Similarly, a difficult situation may remain unchanged, but the feelings associated with it can undergo a transformation. All we need to do is replace negative energy with positive energy.

For example, What can I learn from this situation? What is positive about this situation?

As we make this paradigm shift, our tone and emotions change. We can transition from our current state of mind to a more desired state filled with new possibilities. This helps us gain a 360-degree view of our current reality.

→ What happens when you gain a 360-degree view of your current reality?

→ What happens when the feelings associated with the situation change?

You relax; there is no tension in your muscles, and you gain clarity in thinking. This is the time when you can start exploring different solutions and ideas. This clear thinking will pave the way for you to find the correct path to the solution.

You can also reframe by thinking of your current problem as a challenge statement. Redefining the word 'problem' into a 'challenge statement' helps you perceive life differently.

A few years ago, while driving at a traffic-heavy junction, the driver of the car in front of me suddenly applied the brakes. My car bumped into his car's bumper, denting my number plate. Initially, I was irritated and approached the driver, ready to express my frustration. However, as I got closer, I noticed that the driver was a pregnant woman, likely in her 7th or 8th month of pregnancy. In a split second, I reframed my thoughts and asked her politely, "Are you okay, madam?"

I am not sure how this reframing happened; it just occurred instinctively. It helped avoid conflict, stress, and tension for both of us. The next day, I went to the mechanic to fix my car's number plate without holding any grudges against the lady.

When we consciously pause to reflect before taking action, we often realize that the root cause of sudden outbursts of anger is likely a pain. fear of the unknown, uncertainty, or ridicule. Reframing our thoughts can help the other person disengage. However, implementing this change requires effort and commitment, but the rewards are worth it.

By changing our frame of reference and looking at the same situation from a different perspective, we can alter our responses. Shifting our perspective can lead to changes in our emotional states and behaviors in an instant.

Chapter 7

Six steps in Reframing

I would like to introduce the six sequential steps of the reframing framework based on the work of Neuro-Linguistic Programming (NLP) practitioners. For some, this may take a while, while for others, it could take just a few minutes. With practice, you will be able to master this art.

- Identifying the context where the challenge/problem/behavior/pattern occurred.

- Establishing unconscious yes/no signals.

- Confirming that the problem has a positive 'intent.'

- Finding several ways to fulfill the positive intent.

- Selecting the best possible alternatives.

- Checking that the selection is ecological, meaning it is acceptable to the individual and in relation to others.

Contextual Reframing

The meaning of any problem/situation/event exists only in relation to the context in which it occurs.

Every problem/challenge/situation that occurs could be appropriate in some context. With a context reframe, you could ask:

- Where could this challenge/situation/behavior be useful?
- In what other context would having this problem be valuable?

For example, if you have a habit of procrastinating, can you apply this quality:

→ When you want to enjoy an extra helping of cake?

→ When you are angry and about to lose your temper?

Value Reframing

In brand management and marketing terms, value reframing means assigning new value to a product/service by finding a new market/context. At the heart of the process is the ability to make a linguistic distinction between the intention of the person and their behavior. Doing this allows you to discover newer, more appropriate behaviors. Often, people do not change simply because they have not considered the possibility of an alternative.

To summarize, reframing means

→ Firstly, stepping back from what is being said and done and considering the frame or 'lens' through which reality is being created.

→ Secondly, consider 'alternative lenses' to view things differently and challenge the limiting beliefs of the frame.

→ Thirdly, choosing a position (another frame), describing what you see, and attempting to change some of the attributes of the frame to modify the meaning.

→ Finally, checking what the revised frame looks like.

→ You can, for example, reframe:

- A problem as a challenge or an opportunity.

- A weakness as a strength.

- An impossible task as a future task that could become a possibility.

- A future or distant possibility as a near possibility.

- Procrastination as a method that can be used for different purposes.

It is said that necessity is the mother of invention, but this is not always the case. In fact, some great inventions resulted from happy accidents. When we consider how useful some everyday products are, it is hard to imagine that they were discovered by accident. From potato chips to life-saving X-ray images and penicillin, all of these were unintentionally discovered by individuals on alternative quests.

Let me list out some inventions made by mistake

Potato Chips

In 1853, in a New York restaurant, a customer complained that the fried potatoes were too soggy and thick, repeatedly sending them back to the waiter. The chef, George Crum, became so frustrated that he took the request for thinner potatoes quite literally—he cut the potatoes into thin slices, fried them, and covered them in salt. And yes, the world's most favorite snack was born!

Microwave Oven

In 1945, Percy Spencer was working with a microwave-emitting magnetron when he felt an odd sizzling sensation, and a chocolate bar in his pocket started melting. Utilizing this new knowledge, he patented the microwave.

Cornflakes

The Kellogg brothers, John and Will, discovered the staple breakfast cereal when they accidentally left a pot of boiled grain on the stove for several days.

Non-Stick Pans (Teflon)

If you're cooking food in non-stick pans, it is thanks to chemist Roy Plunkett. Long before CFCs (Chlorofluorocarbons) became the environmental super-villains depleting the ozone layer, Plunkett was aiming to create a new type of chlorofluorocarbon. But this experiment turned out to be the high melting point lubricant now consistently applied to all non-stick pans. Teflon was first used in military applications and is now famously applied to cookware around the world.

LSD

The psychoactive properties of acid were discovered almost by accident by Dr. Albert Hofmann, a research chemist working for the Sandoz Company, in 1943. Dr. Hofmann had been synthesizing LSD-25, and some crystals of the substance made contact with his fingertips and were absorbed through his skin.

Matchsticks

In 1826, British chemist John Walker discovered what matchsticks were when he accidentally scraped a stick coated in chemicals across his hearth and found that it caught fire. The idea struck him to convert these into proper matchsticks.

Safety Glass

In 1903, chemist Edward Benedictus was working in his lab when he accidentally knocked over a flask. However, when Benedictus looked down, he noticed that instead of breaking into a million little pieces, the glassware had just cracked slightly while maintaining its shape. After further investigation, the scientist learned that what had kept the glass together was a cellulose nitrate coating inside the glass, and thus safety glass was created.

X-Ray Images

In 1895, a physics professor, Wilhelm Conrad Röntgen, was working on a cathode ray tube when he shielded the tube with thick paper and discovered a fluorescent light generated by a material located near the tube. He concluded that a new type of ray was being emitted from the tube. Further investigation soon found that the new ray could pass through most substances while casting shadows on solid objects, paving the way for X-rays as we know them.

Coca-Cola

Atlanta-based pharmacist John Pemberton capitalized on the trend by selling a French wine-coca concoction that was touted as a cure for headaches and nervous disorders. Pemberton's business hit a speed bump in 1885 when Atlanta banned the sale of alcohol, so he omitted the wine and created a coca-based syrup that could be mixed with carbonated water and drunk as a soda. He named this new 'valuable brain tonic' Coca-Cola, which was said to cure headaches, relieve exhaustion, and calm nerves.

Brandy

A Dutch shipmaster was trying to make wine easier to transport and decided to use heat to concentrate the alcohol, planning to add water to it once he arrived at his destination.

However, he discovered that the taste of concentrated wine was much better than that of watered-down wine. So, he forewent the water part of his plan and called his new alcohol 'Brandewijn,' meaning 'burnt wine' in Dutch.

Viagra

The sildenafil compound was originally developed by Pfizer for the treatment of hypertension and angina pectoris. During the clinical trials for heart-related issues, researchers discovered that the drug was more effective at inducing erections than treating angina.

Slinky

Naval engineer Richard James was trying to develop a spring that would support and stabilize sensitive equipment on ships. When one of the springs accidentally fell off a shelf, it continued moving, and James got the idea for a toy. His wife, Betty, came up with the name, and when the Slinky made its debut in late 1945, James sold 400 of the bouncy toys in 90 minutes.

Ink-Jet Printers

According to Business Insider, a Canon engineer accidentally left a hot iron on his ink pen. Due to heat pressure, the ink pen almost started dropping ink from its point. Hence, the incident gave him the idea to create inkjet printers.

Source: Article from Concordia University

Reframing means looking at situations and challenges differently in a context that allows us to learn and understand the positive aspects. If we can accept whatever life gives us and view situations as opportunities rather than difficulties or problems, we can make the most of the reframing techniques. Many difficulties and problems can be reframed into situations and challenges that help us become holistic humans.

All we need to do is keep trusting ourselves, our ability to implement the paradigm shift, reframe, and set positive outcomes.

Chapter 8

A Study on Reframing

A farmer had a beloved horse that helped the family earn a living. One day, the horse ran away, and his neighbors exclaimed, 'Your horse ran away, What terrible luck!'

The farmer replied, 'Maybe so, maybe not.'

A few days later, the horse returned home, leading a few wild horses back to the farm as well. The neighbors shouted, 'Your horse has returned, and he brought several horses home with him. What great luck!'

The farmer replied, 'Maybe so, maybe not.'

Later that week, the farmer's son tried to ride one of the horses, and she threw him to the ground, breaking his leg. The neighbors cried, 'Your son broke his leg; what terrible luck!'

The farmer replied, 'Maybe so, maybe not.'

A few weeks later, soldiers from the national army marched through town, mandatorily recruiting all young boys for the army. They did not take the farmer's son because he had a broken leg. The neighbors shouted, 'Your boy is spared; what tremendous luck!'

To which the farmer replied, 'Maybe so, maybe not.'

When something happens, it is impossible to tell whether it is good or bad. You never know what the consequences will be, as only time will tell the whole story. Things may look great in the beginning; however, over time, they may not be what you had imagined. Similarly, you may feel negative about something, and someday it could prove to be one of the best things that ever happened to you.

Activity 1

Write down one personal and one professional instance in your life like this example.

Activity 2

Please observe in your daily life: Some more examples of things you can control and influence

What is in your Control?

- → Your happiness
- → Delayed flight
- → Getting stuck in traffic
- → Late in offering birthday wishes to a colleague
- → An angry friend shouting at you
- → Your upbringing

What is not in your Control?

Though the above may not be in your control, the way you respond/react to the above situations is definitely in your control.

Chapter 9

Contaminated Vocabulary

The choice of the words that we use to communicate with ourselves and others also impacts our thinking and results. There are certain words that need to be carefully handled when thinking in outcomes.

I remember my first seminar on an introduction to NLP, more than twenty-five years ago, where the seminar leader was teaching us the power of language.

Not only did I understand that specific words affect our mental pictures, but I also understood that words are a powerful programming factor in lifelong success.

The seminar leader was sharing a story of his childhood days with us. Let me share this with you verbatim, as I heard it from him.

One particularly interesting event occurred when I was eight. As a child, I was always climbing trees and poles and literally hanging upside down from the rafters of our lake house. So, it came as no surprise for my dad to find me one day, at the top of a 30-foot tree, swinging back and forth. My little eight-year-old brain didn't realize that the tree could break or that I could get hurt. I just thought it was fun to be up so high. My friend John was also on the tree. He was hanging on the first big limb, about ten feet below me. John's mother noticed us at the exact same time as my father. About that time, a huge gust of wind blew over the tree.

I heard the leaves starting to rattle, and the tree began to sway. I remember my dad's voice over the wind yelling, "Son, hold on tightly." So I did.

The next thing I knew... I heard John screaming at the top of his lungs, lying flat on the ground. He had fallen out of the tree. I scampered down the tree to safety. My dad later told me why he fell, and I did not. Apparently, John's mother was not as astute as my father. When John's mother felt the gust of wind, she yelled out, "John, don't fall!"

And guess what? John did fall.

My dad then explained to me that the mind has a very difficult time processing a negative image. In fact, people who rely on internal pictures cannot see the negative at all. For John to process the command to not fall, his nine-year-old brain had to first imagine falling, then try to tell the brain not to do what it had just imagined. Whereas, my eight-year-old brain instantly had an internal image of me "hanging on tightly".

That's why people who try to stop smoking struggle with the act of quitting. They picture themselves smoking all day. Smokers are rarely taught to see themselves breathing fresh air and feeling great. The language itself becomes a barrier to success. This concept is especially useful when you are attempting to break a habit or set a goal.

You can't visualize not doing something. The only way to properly visualize NOT doing something is to find a word for what you want to do and visualize that. For example, when I was about twelve years old, I used to play gully cricket, just like many of the boys at that age in India, do. I tried so hard to be good, but I just couldn't get it together at that age. I remember during a game of cricket, while I was fielding, the words of a senior boy ran through my head as I was running to take a catch, 'Don't drop it!' Naturally, I dropped the ball.

My coaches (the elderly boys in our apartment complex) were not skilled enough to give me proper 'self-talk'. They just thought that some kids could catch and others couldn't. I could never become a pro, but I am now a pretty good Sunday afternoon cricket player, playing with my second son, because all my internal dialogue is positive. It encourages me to catch the ball at the right time. I wish I had learned the art of positive self-talk then. Perhaps I could have played cricket for my school, college or even university

Ask yourself: How many compliments do you give yourself every day versus how many criticisms? (I know you are talking to yourself all day long.) We all have internal voices that give us direction. So, are you giving yourself the 17:1 ratio or are you shortchanging yourself with toxic self-talk like, 'I suck, I am fat, nobody will like me, I will try this diet, I am not good enough, I am so stupid, I am broke,' etc.?

If our parents can set a lifetime of programming with one wrong statement, imagine the kind of programming you are doing daily with your own internal dialogue.

Here is a summary list of contaminated Vocabulary words. Notice when you or other people use them.

But
Try
If
Might
Would have
Don't
Could have
Can't
Should have

The functions of these words are:

Words	Functions
But	negates any words that are stated before it
If	presupposes that you may not
Would have	past tense that draws attention to things that didn't happen
Should have	past tense that draws attention to things that didn't happen (implies guilt)
Could have	past tense that draws attention to things that didn't happen, but the person takes credit as if it did happen
Try	presupposes failure

Words	Functions
Might	It does nothing definite and keeps options open for your listener
Can't/ Don't	These words force the listener to focus on exactly the opposite of what you want. This is a mistake many coaches, managers and facilitators make without knowing how much damage this linguistic error can do

Examples

Toxic Phrases

Words	Likely Result	Better Phrases
Don't drop the ball	Drops the ball	Catch the ball
You shouldn't watch so much TV	Watches more TV	I read that too much TV makes our brains lazy. You may find yourself turning that TV off and picking up one of those good books more often

Exercise

Take a moment to write down all the phrases you use daily or any toxic self-talk that you have noticed yourself using. Write these phrases down so that you will begin to catch yourself as they occur and change them.

Chapter 10

The Six Ps of Reframing

As you have read in the previous chapter, everyone sees and understands things differently. As the old saying goes, beauty lies in the eyes of the beholder. Similarly, knowledge too often lies in the eye of the beholder.

The Six Ps of reframing enable different perspectives to be generated and used in management processes. This helps expand the number of options for solving problems and determining outcomes.

1. Programme Perspective

2. Planning Perspective

3. People Perspective

4. Process Perspective

5. Product Perspective

6. Potential Perspective

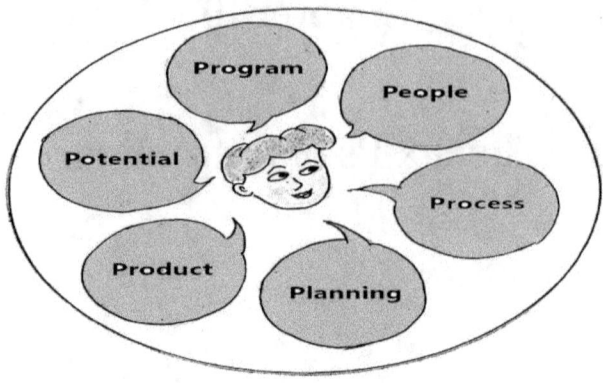

Here are a few sample questions for each P that could help you in your journey of finding a path to solutions.

Programme Perspective

→ What practices are being advocated?

- What current practices do you adopt?
- What practices does your department/organisation adopt?
- How do you practice these?

→ What are the benefits?

- What benefits do you derive from the above practices?
- What benefits have your customers derived from these practices?

→ Are they simple to use?
→ Are they correctly targeted?

- Is this targeted at the right audience?

Planning Perspective

- Does the implementation plan make sense?
- Is the timing correct?
- What other deadlines block this?

People Perspective

- How do different employees/teams see this tool/plan?
- Have you checked with each employee/your team members about this?
- How does your customer see this?
- How will your competitors see this?
- How will your collaborative partners look at this?
- What do they think of the strategy?

Process Perspective

- What are the series of actions that you do for a particular function/situation/event?
- What are the different changes that happen or can happen naturally?
- How do you deal with information?
- How does your team deal with information?
- What are the progressive as well as independent steps?
- What different methods have been adopted or need to be adopted to create value?

Product Perspective

- How is your product evolving/how will your product evolve?
- How do you want your product to evolve?

- How would your customers want your products to evolve?
- How would your partners want your products to evolve?
- How would your competitors want your products to evolve?
- How specifically is your product/service aligned with your company's mission/vision?
- Are any parts of your product or services misaligned with your company's vision or mission?
- If yes, then what do you plan to change?
→ How is your product/service solving your customers' needs/problems?
- How specifically does your product or service address your customer's needs?

Potential Perspective

→ Is our analysis of the potential value of the practices accurate?
- What are the gaps in our analysis?
→ How do we continue to increase the use of tools?
- What steps or approaches do you want to adopt to increase the use of the tools?
→ What other opportunities are available?
- What opportunities are available now?
- What opportunities can be made available in the future?
- Are these opportunities available here or outside your organisation?

Thus, reframing is a brief, deliberate re-direction that temporarily shifts focus to the higher-level question of how the problem is framed. It results in a new or improved understanding of the problem.

Source: 'Some Aspects of the Six Ps'adapted from Ben Ramalingam, 2006.

Tools for Knowledge and Learning: A Guide for Development and Humanitarian Organizations, Overseas Development Institute.

Chapter 11

The Perception of Reality Map

When you perceive a challenge, you perceive its reality map. People usually respond to their map of reality and not to reality itself.

Does this mean that the problem is not real?

Maybe yes, or maybe not.

In the phrase coined by Alfred Korzybski in his book 'Science and Sanity,' published in 1933, 'the map is not the territory.' You need to master the art of changing your map to one that gives you more choices. It works like the wise man in the famous story of the 17 camels:

A father left 17 camels as an asset for his three sons. When the father passed away, his sons looked up his will. It stated that the eldest son should get half of the 17 camels, while the middle son should be given one-third, and the youngest son should be given one-ninth of the 17 camels. As it was not possible to divide 17 into equal halves, thirds, or ninths, the three sons started fighting with each other. They decided to seek the counsel of a wise man.

The wise man listened patiently to the details of the will. After giving it some thought, he brought one camel of his own and added it to the 17. This increased the total to 18 camels. Now he began interpreting the deceased father's will.

½ of 18 = 9. So, he gave the eldest son 9 camels. 1/3rd of 18 = 6. So, he gave the middle son 6 camels. 1/9th of 18 = 2. So, he gave the youngest son 2 camels.

Now, if we add this up: 9 plus 6 plus 2, the total is 17, leaving one camel, which the wise man took back.

The 18th camel story may seem magical and perhaps too simple. Sometimes, the solution is simple. To find the solution, however, the parties must be willing to collaborate to discover their real interests. Additionally, they must prefer using a joint problem-solving approach rather than a method based on 'demands, confrontation, and concession,' which at best leads to compromise.

The attitude of negotiation and problem-solving is to find the 18th camel, i.e., the common ground. Once a person can find common ground, the issue is resolved. It is challenging at times, but to reach a solution, the first step is to believe that there is one. If we think that there is no solution, we will not be able to find any!

It is interesting how much this story resembles many of the difficult negotiations we get involved in. They start off like seemingly unsolvable problems, much like dividing 17 camels. What we need to do is step back from the situation, as the wise old man did, look at it with fresh eyes, and come up with an 18th camel.

What solution do you have to offer to the desperate situations around you?

What comfort or resolution can your wisdom and generosity bring to those who come across your path?

Are you riding on the 18th camel?

When confronted with a challenging problem, remember the 18th camel and come up with an innovative solution.

- How do you create a map of a problem/challenge?
- How do you determine whether it is real or not?

Let us understand how this map is built.

You perceive the problem through your five senses. So, the way you perceive your problem depends on which particular sense is strongest in you. How you use your senses affects your thinking, and the good news is that you can change your experience by altering how you use your senses. When you change your thoughts about a business challenge or personal problem by re-communicating through your five senses, your knowledge and understanding will be completely different.

You represent your experiences to yourself using only your 5 senses, and these can be termed as representational systems.

1. Sight   (visual - V)
2. Sound   (auditory - A)
3. Touch/Feeling   (kinaesthetic - K)
4. Taste   (gustatory - G)
5. Smell   (olfactory - O)

When an organization encounters a business challenge, the person who perceives this problem through the auditory system needs to learn and acknowledge how other team members use their respective senses to experience it. This will enable the department to gain a 360-degree holistic view of the problem and be aware of how different people perceive it in various ways. This paves the way for finding the solution.

For example, consider individuals who rely more on their feelings and emotions. The kinesthetic system encompasses feelings of balance (the vestibule system), bodily sensations from within, and direct tactile sensations from the outside. It also includes emotions and feelings about people or situations, which are clusters of feelings in the body that can be labeled, such as fright, anxiety, love, and hate.

You may have noticed that some people, while working on a specific situation or problem, suddenly develop a headache, a body ache, or some kind of pain. This is because they sense the business problem through their kinaesthetic senses.

Every moment, you create your internal world using representation systems. Once you understand that you create your internal world, you can start shaping it the way you want it, rather than relying on your brain's default settings.

Just as we develop skills and preferences for using our senses externally, we do the same with our representation systems internally.

Ask yourself: What are your preferences?

With a visual preference, you may be able to perceive the problem differently; you can visualize the problem's origin, who it affects, and how your clients perceive this challenge. Perhaps, when you examine the problem visually, you can see different dimensions of it, including its colour, shape, and size. All these could provide you with clues about where to find the path to a solution.

Similarly, if you have an auditory preference, you may hear voices in your mind or want to hear how the problem sounds. By paying close attention to the direction of sound, you may gain insights into the problem's causes.

The more you use your kinesthetic senses externally and the more acute they become, the more you may favour them as representation systems internally. When you start feeling the problem from within, you can sense the stress, pain, and tremendous strength needed to address it. Identifying which part of your body is affected when you think about this problem, along with its intensity and depth, could provide clues about the problem's nature, its side effects, and the approach required to tackle it.

When you recreate an experience, you are likely to use one of the sensory systems as the lead system. If it is the visual system, it acts like an icon. You can click on it, and the entire visual representation of your problem can open up with its divisions, parts, accessories, and by-products. Examine it widely to gain greater clarity about your problem.

Likewise, an auditory lead system is akin to hearing the first few notes of a piece of music and instantly recognizing it. Listen to the sounds associated with your problem, including finer nuances like notes, volumes, pitch, and octaves. This comprehensive approach can provide a full view and sound like a home theater or Dolby stereo system where you can clearly hear every instrument being played, helping you better understand your problem.

A kinesthetic lead system transports you back to your complete memory of the problem, allowing you to feel how it happened and how deeply it affected you. You can sense the pain associated with this unresolved issue. When using your kinaesthetic senses, pay attention to the finer nuances of the problem's parts, such as where it causes discomfort, the depth and intensity of pressure, and the reasons behind these sensations. This information can provide valuable insights into the problem's depth and potentially lead you to the source where it initially occurred, paving the way for solutions.

For individuals with a predominant olfactory or gustatory sense, they may perceive a problem's fragrance or taste. You might wonder how a business problem could have a smell or taste. What this means is not why the problem should have a smell or taste, but how does it smell or taste to you? This may not apply to individuals who lack a leading or supporting sense of olfactory or gustatory. This paragraph is relevant only to those who internally communicate through smell and taste when facing a situation. For example, someone might smell a book before buying it, or when confronted with a situation, they may notice a change in their taste or saliva production. These signals serve as a method of communication. What matters is how you communicate with yourself and which sense predominates.

Through these sensory approaches, you can gain a clearer assessment of the problem, better understand it, articulate it conveniently, and begin to chart a path toward a solution.

Chapter 12

Metaphor

Metaphors exist halfway between the unintelligible and the commonplace. They encompass figures of speech, stories, comparisons, similes, and parables. Metaphors enable subtle or obvious comparisons and connections. To comprehend our experiences, we rely on making comparisons.

Place your fingertips on the nearest surface and observe the information you gather through your sense of touch. Now, slowly run your fingers along it. You will encounter various tactile sensations, and through comparisons, you can discern much about the surface's character, texture, and temperature.

Stories are an inherent part of our lives, and metaphors permeate our thinking. They are interwoven into our existence at every level, from the bedtime stories of our childhood to the ways we contemplate work, life, relationships, and health. Metaphors forge creative connections between two events or experiences, providing an alternative and hopefully enlightening interpretation. Religious leaders, politicians, and business figures paradoxically employ metaphors and parables to enhance the clarity of their ideas.

Look at this example:

How would you complete this, and what would that mean?

Life is like

a battle?

a bowl of cherries?

a struggle?

an adventure?

The metaphors a person employs provide the 'key' to their life and thought processes. Someone who sees life as an adventure approaches events differently from someone who views life as a struggle.

Organizations also utilize metaphors. An organization that values teamwork will respond differently than one that perceives itself as a combat force. Currently, a common metaphor for businesses is 'A Learning Organization,' which evokes a distinct image. Some organizations still identify as family businesses, a potent metaphor reflecting their values and employee treatment.

Interestingly, the financial world is replete with liquid metaphors. Phrases like cash flow, flooding the market, liquid and frozen assets, and floating a company are common. Money is often likened to water, perhaps?

The field of medicine and healthcare is rife with metaphors, not all of them promoting health. We speak of waging war against COVID, cancer, fighting illness, and eradicating germs. Our immune system and physiological identity are often portrayed as killing machines. Effectiveness is equated with health, while breakdown results in illness. Alternatively, more constructive health metaphors revolve around balance, working with the body, and coexistence.

Metaphors are not inherently right or wrong, but they influence how people think and act, with implications embedded within them. Now, let us explore solving business challenges or problems using metaphors.

In metaphors, people and experiences need not be strictly one thing or the other; they can embody both or neither. The sum of one and one is not always two; it can also be one. For instance, one and one can equal one when they are raindrops or nil when they are black holes. One plus one can even equal three when two people build a family.

Milton Erickson, one of the greatest hypnotherapists, used to share stories with his clients. These stories would begin somewhat similarly to the client's problem but end with a resolution. The link between the two would hold the key to resolving the problem.

Instructing people on what to do doesn't always work because they are already aware of it, and it resides in their conscious mind as information. A metaphor transcends conscious understanding.

For instance, a therapist worked with a married couple facing relationship difficulties. While they wished to remain together, cooperation proved challenging.

The therapist suggested they take dancing lessons as a metaphor for their relationship. Both had some prior dancing experience, although not with each other. Through dancing, they learned the dynamics of give and take, ebb and flow, lead and follow—qualities they had been missing in their relationship. Metaphors wield significant power in relationships, influencing how we treat our partners. Marriage, for example, can be seen as a battle of the sexes, a union, a sacred vow, or peaceful coexistence.

Ask yourself the following questions:

- What metaphor am I living?

- A tale of self-sacrifice?

- A heroic quest?

- What sort of film would it make?

- A comedy or a tragedy?

Once upon a time...

We need stories. They are so important that we tell ourselves half a dozen while we sleep every night, even though we don't always remember them. These dreams often appear strange to our conscious minds, yet they can be incredibly creative. Stories are such an integral part of our daily lives that we sometimes forget their immense power. When we return home from work or school and switch on the television, we are greeted with stories.

Have you ever heard them say, '... and the top news story today is...?'

Modern-day technology continues to deliver stories to us. The computer itself is often seen as a metaphor for the brain.

Chapter 13

Problem-Solving
through metaphors

As you understand metaphors better, let us do an activity. Jot down the following:

Think of your current business challenge or problem. How would you describe it as a metaphor?

Your problem is like...

a jam sandwich?
a ringing phone?
a card game?
a fight with a monster?
being stranded on a deserted island?

→ This is your present state.

→ Now, let's focus on your metaphor.

→ What are the assumptions inherent in that metaphor?

→ What else would have to be true for that metaphor to be accurate?

- Now think of what you would prefer the problem to be like and think of another metaphor.

- I would prefer...

- Now think about what the problem is like.

- What are the differences between the first metaphor and the second metaphor?

- How could you get from one to the other?

- How are they similar?

- The connection could be the resource that helps you find a path to a solution.

Chapter 14

D
R
Ideation
V
E

Ideation forms an important part of the drive framework which helps you to reach your desired outcome.

The focus of this book is to help you arrive at a desired state and to emphasize the identification of problem areas, assist you in making the right decisions, and guide you toward finding the correct solutions. To better comprehend this, it is essential to understand what ideation is, why you need it, and where, when, and how to apply it. Based on these considerations, you can employ various approaches to navigate toward a solution. However, it is crucial to grasp the process of ideation itself before delving into problem-solving mode.

According to the Oxford Dictionary, ideation is the process of forming ideas from conception to implementation, most often in a business context. Ideation is expressed through graphical, written, or verbal methods and emerges from past or present knowledge, influences, opinions, experiences, and personal convictions.

For this process to succeed, we must start from the beginning by identifying the mental blocks that hinder ideation.

Let us identify some of the mental blocks that hinder ideation

1. <u>Defining challenges</u>

Challenges are often narrowly defined, limiting our perspective and preventing the generation of comprehensive ideas, resulting in suboptimal solutions.

2. <u>Viewing the problem from only one perspective</u>

We interact with the world through our senses. Restricting our perception to just one sense can hinder our understanding of challenges. To overcome this, we should aim to observe, listen to, feel, smell, and even taste the challenge.

3. <u>Seeking a single answer</u>

Is there always just one answer? Many people search for a single solution to a problem or a multitude of problems. However, the answer found may not be the right one or the best solution. During ideation, it is essential not to limit your thinking to a single solution but to explore a variety of options that can lead you down the right path.

4. <u>Insisting on strict logic</u>

Relying solely on logic may not address some challenges. Creativity often exists beyond the bounds of strict logic.

At times, it is necessary to approach challenges from a non-logical perspective.

5. Fearing failure

Fear of failure is a common roadblock when ideating or aiming to be creative. Many individuals shy away from failure. It is important to recognize that there are no failures, only feedback and unintended results.

6. Conforming to group pressures

Often when we start working on solutions, due to group pressures we often neglect to go in depth of ideation and rush to arrive at a solution thus jumping the queue to reach the solution. (next line) Therefore, for ideas/solutions to be effective, the following need to be taken in to account

- Stating the challenge/problem broadly

- Considering many viewpoints

- Continuing to look for additional answers

- Inspecting the rules to see if the reason behind the logic still exists

- Suspending logic temporarily

- Suspending judgment

- Looking at the reality of the problem

Chapter 15

D
R
I
Validation
E

The next and most important part of the DRIVE framework is Validation. The purpose of validation is to make sure your business idea has potential and the most critical assumptions regarding your idea are valid.

Validation is the process of collecting and evaluating data, starting from the process design stage through production, to establish scientific evidence that a process and/or device can consistently deliver a quality product.

Why validate?

Validating the accuracy, clarity, and details of data is essential to mitigating potential project defects. Without data validation, there is a risk of making decisions based on inaccurate information. An organization comprises various functions, teams, and individuals working collaboratively. Different team members may propose various ideas/solutions to a given problem or challenge. Naturally, not all ideas can be considered equally valuable. Therefore, the need for validation and selection arises.

What to validate?

Anything can be subject to validation. For instance, you can validate someone's response, your own speech, writings, comments, or the root cause of an incident.

In our context, after ideation, it becomes necessary to validate ideas to shortlist the top few. On an average, the human mind can generate twenty ideas in two minutes. So, if you engage in group ideation to address a business challenge, you might generate approximately 20-50 ideas. Therefore, validation plays a crucial role in this process.

What are the methods of validation?

Organizations and individuals around the world employ various methods to validate their ideas, processes, systems, and products. One highly beneficial method is the use of powerful questions to validate an idea, project, or solution. This is also mentioned as part of the chapter 18

Chapter 16

The Six Steps of Validation

Let us take a deeper dive into the exact validation steps. Once you have shortlisted the top three/five ideas, further filtration is necessary before making a final decision. While this may be somewhat time-consuming, it is crucial to complete this process before reaching a final decision. This step is essential for mitigating potential challenges that could impede the growth and future prospects of the business.

1. **Deciding** - Identifying the Decision: Sometimes, the main challenge is forgotten, and people deviate from the actual issue due to the sheer number of ideas generated during the ideation session. It is essential to refocus thoughts on the identified decision. For instance, the identified decision could be one of the solutions that you or your team might have discussed, such as improving employee retention by 25%, introducing a four-day workweek, or increasing gender diversity by 30%.

2. **Data Mining** - Gathering Relevant Information: Data mining involves sorting through extensive datasets to identify patterns and relationships that can help address business challenges. It is the process of sifting through

information during ideation to identify emerging patterns. Different teams may generate ideas with distinct patterns due to variations in their data research methods. it is crucial to gather necessary and relevant information, as relevance varies from one organization or department to another. Finding patterns is vital during this information gathering process to ensure a bias-free and unbiased approach.

3. **Optioning** - Identifying and Evaluating Alternatives: Many organizations go through the entire ideation process and generate brilliant ideas. However, due to a lack of validation, these ideas are sometimes implemented without proper scrutiny, leading to potential issues. It is advisable to have a Plan B in case Plan A doesn't produce the desired results, preventing resource waste.

4. **Weightage** - Evaluating the Evidence: This step involves emotionally participating and cognitively appreciating what each idea's implementation would entail. To evaluate evidence non-judgmentally, it is essential to utilize emotional intelligence. During this process, imagine using each alternative to its conclusion to visualize the potential outcomes.

5. **Selecting** - Choosing among the Alternatives: Selecting the best alternative can be a challenging task, especially when working as a team with multiple ideas. When making a selection, remain impartial and consider potential issues, risks, and obstacles associated with each alternative.

6. **Reviewing** - Evaluating your decision and its Consequences: People generally make choices based on the available information at a given moment. After completing the previous five steps, it is important to review your decision and its potential consequences. Ask questions such as,

'What did we miss?'

'Where did we go wrong?' and

'Can we afford any risks with this choice?'

This thorough evaluation helps mitigate future risks associated with the decision.

In conclusion, following these six validation steps can lead to better decision - making and minimize potential challenges or setbacks in the future.

Chapter 17

D
R
I
V
Experimenting

The last step in the DRIVE framework after reviewing the next step after reviewing the decision and its consequences is experimentation. Without experimentation, you may not fully understand the impact of your ideation and validation processes. Taking positive action through experimentation puts you in control of the situation.

How do you go about this?

After completing the review process, jot down a couple of sentences describing your goal, and then break that goal into smaller, attainable steps.

Through experimentation, you can enhance customer expectations. More customers are drawn to service providers or manufacturers who consistently experiment with their products and services.

As you are already aware, this book emphasizes Outcome Thinking, so the first and foremost step is to envision an outcome that will:

1. Improve the customer experience and retain customers. The more you experiment, the better the customer experience becomes.

2. Ensure that the experiment is data-driven throughout. Without data, your experiment may yield suboptimal results. Even after ideation, you may need to collect authentic data supported by evidence and research.

3. Keep an open mind. After going through the process of defining, refining, and ideating, make sure your mind remains open.

4. Improve inclusion, diversity, and equity. Working with a diverse team adds value, although it can bring challenges. During experimentation, listening to each other and encouraging every team member produces better results than allowing team members to work in isolation. Experimenting with a team from diverse backgrounds, cultures, experiences, and knowledge leads to impactful results. An empowered team performs better in experimentation and all other aspects of work.

5. Invest in the right tools. A team that invests in the right tools achieves desired results. Choose tools based on your area of interest or the challenge you are addressing.

6. Celebrate success. In many organizations, teams may not receive adequate appreciation or rewards after

experimentation or task completion. Rewards need not always be monetary; a simple acknowledgment or a pat on the back at the right time acknowledges the team's success and leadership. Celebrate even small successes; you do not have to wait for the final outcome. During interim periods when you have broken down the main goal into sub-tasks, celebrating the completion of each task boosts team morale, energizes team members, and enhances their confidence. Celebrating success, whether big or small, is crucial.

7. Understand that there are no failures; only feedback. Often, we are conditioned to view failure negatively from a young age. This leads to fear when we encounter failure or do not achieve our desired outcomes. Let us adopt a different approach and replace the term 'failure' with 'feedback.' In all our endeavors, we receive results, which may be desired or undesired. Reserve the term 'failure' for inanimate objects like pens or electronic devices. In relationships and human endeavors, no one truly fails; they receive feedback indicating that their approach has produced different results than desired. This different outcome is simply termed 'feedback.'

When you experiment, you always gather results or feedback. When you receive an undesired result that does not align with your desired outcome, view it as feedback.

Reevaluate your process or steps, and consider what you might have missed. Change your approach if necessary. If you keep using the same approach, you will keep getting the same results. To achieve different outcomes, adjust your approach and choose the path that leads to your desired results. Shift your perspective and see failure as feedback. Remember, no one truly fails; they continually receive feedback.

When setting realistic goals, it is essential to view success and feedback through different lenses.

Chapter 18

Powerful Questions Framework

You may also use the following powerful question framework after experimenting:

- Did your solution/experiment have a direct and/or material effect on the quality of life?
- Did it address a compelling need?
- Did it solve a compelling problem?
- Was it a fresh breakthrough?
- Was there a "WOW" factor?
- Did it change the way business is conducted?
- Did it increase the efficiency of how resources are used?
- Did it spark an ongoing stream of innovations?
- Did it lead to the creation of a vast, new industry?

- The End -

I am sure you enjoyed reading this book and were able to complete all the activities mentioned. If not please complete the activities which will help you to enhance your capability as well as confidence in addressing any challenges in life or at work. Happy outcome thinking.

K V Vishwanathan

THE WRITE ORDER

You Write. We Publish.

To publish your own book, contact us.

We publish poetry collections, short story collections, novellas and novels.

contact@thewriteorder.com

Instagram- thewriteorder

www.facebook.com/thewriteorder

www.ingramcontent.com/pod-product-compliance
Lightning Source LLC
LaVergne TN
LVHW010400070526
838199LV00065B/5866